W0010440

ALASKA
in words and pictures

BY DENNIS B. FRADIN

ILLUSTRATIONS BY ROBERT ULM

Consultant
Diana Murphy
Travel Information Officer

FAIRVIEW SOUTH
LIBRARY
SKOKIE, ILLINOIS 60076

CHILDRENS PRESS ™
CHICAGO

16262
917.98
FRA

Barrow
Artic Ocean
Prudhoe Bay
Kotzebue
Canada
Nome
☐ State or territorial Highway
Yukon R.
Fairbanks
Mt. McKinley
2 Alaska Highway
1
Willow
Anchorage
Valdez
Skagway
Seward
JUNEAU
Gulf of Alaska
Sitka
Pribilof Islands
Wrangell
Ketchikan
Kodiak Island
Bering Sea

Attu Island
Aleutian Islands
Bering Sea
Alaska Peninsula
Alaska Peninsula

Library of Congress Cataloging in Publication Data

Fradin, Dennis.
  Alaska in words and pictures.

  SUMMARY: A brief introduction to the geography,
history, natural resources, and people of Alaska.
  1. Alaska—Juvenile literature. [1. Alaska]
I. Ulm, Robert. II. Title.
F904.3.F72   979.8   77-4353
ISBN 0-516-03902-4

Copyright© 1977 by Regensteiner Publishing Enterprises, Inc.
All rights reserved. Published simultaneously in Canada.
Printed in the United States of America.

9 10 11 12 R 85

Picture Acknowledgments:

DEPT. OF INTERIOR: NATIONAL PARK SERVICE PHOTO BY
  FRED KANS—5
DEPT. OF INTERIOR: NATIONAL SERVICE PHOTO BY
  KEITH TREXLER—34
ALASKA DIVISION OF TOURISM—cover, 7, 15, 17 (right), 19, 22,
  24, 25, 26, 27, 29, 32, 33, 35, 36, 38, 39 (left), 40, 43
MEL ANDERSON—8, 13, 17, 31, 41
WIDE WORLD PHOTO—21, 23
SAN DIEGO ZOO—26, 42
JERRY AND IRIS RUDNIK—11, 39
COVER PICTURE—Glacier Bay

Alaska (ah•LASS•kah) comes from the Aleut (ah•LOOT) word *Alyeska* (ALLEY•Es•ka)— meaning "The Great Land." Alaska is the land of Eskimos, reindeer, and polar bears. But it has much more.

Do you know where the largest bears in the world live?

Do you know where the highest mountain in North America is?

Do you know which state grows 70-pound cabbages?

Do you know which state is the largest?

As you will see, the answer to all these questions is The Great Land—Alaska!

Millions of years ago, there were no people on the Great Land. But there were a lot of animals. Moose and caribou (KAIR • ih • boo) lived here. There were also many animals that no longer exist. Giant beavers, woolly mammoths, and saber-toothed tigers ruled the land.

Over a million years ago the weather turned cold. This was the Ice Age. Huge sheets of ice—called *glaciers* (GLAY • sherz)—moved down slowly from the North Pole. A good part of Alaska was covered by glaciers. They dug out valleys. They carved up the coastline.

The glaciers came and went many times during the long Ice Age. Finally, the weather became warmer. The Ice Age was over. In most of North America the glaciers melted. But Alaska's glaciers did not all melt. The summers in Alaska were too short to melt the ice.

That is why you can see so many glaciers in Alaska today.

Moonrise over Nizana Glacier

You know that the first people in America were Indians. Did you ever wonder where they came from? Most scientists think that the Indians came from Asia. One part of Asia is only 54 miles from Alaska. Water separates the two lands.

How did the Indians get to Alaska from Asia? They WALKED! No, they didn't walk over water. Over 20,000 years ago—a strip of land connected Asia and Alaska. Scientists think that the Indians crossed this land bridge as they hunted for meat. From Alaska, the Indians spread all across North America. But some Indians stayed in Alaska.

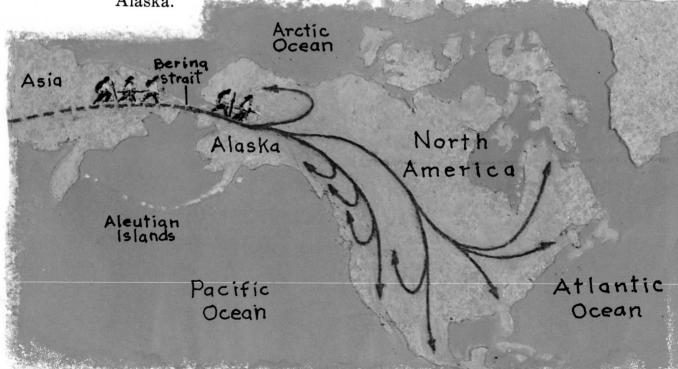

Ketchikan has the biggest collection of totem poles in the world

The Tlingit (TLIN • gt) Indians lived (and still live) in southeastern Alaska. They speared salmon and whales from boats. The Tlingit Indians wove beautiful blankets, which they sometimes used for money. Many Tlingit families had totem poles outside their wood houses. The totem pole told stories—through pictures—about the family. Other totem poles told stories about events important to the village.

The Eskimos (ESS • kih • mohz) lived (and still live) mostly in the far north and west, near the coast. It is believed that the Eskimos also came from Asia, more than 10,000 years ago. But by this time the Land Bridge was covered by water. It is thought that the Eskimos came by boat. Eskimo villages have been found that are 1800 years old. The village of Barrow, where Eskimos still live, is at least 400 years old.

Barrow

Many people think that Eskimos lived in ice houses, called *igloos* (IG•looz). This is not true. The Eskimo word *igloo* means "shelter" or "house." Most igloos were made of wood, dirt, or stone. Once in a while, in the winter, hunters far from home built snow igloos.

Eskimo hunters killed caribou, sheep, and moose on land. For hunting at sea, the Eskimos used special canoes. The *kayak* (KYE•ack), made of wood and skin, was built for one or two. Many could fit into an *umiak* (OOH•me•ack). Eskimos hunted seals, walruses, and whales. In the winter, Eskimos dug holes in the ice to fish through.

The Eskimos used just about every part of the animals they killed. They ate the meat, which they shared, no matter who had killed the animal. They used the fat and oil for cooking, for lighting, and for heating. They carved statues from the walrus tusks. They made warm clothes out of the animal skins. They needed warm clothes. In the frozen north, the temperature can reach 60 degrees below 0!

Eskimos loved to hold great feasts. They played drums, danced, and told stories. Eskimo children played Blanket Toss. In this game they were bounced high into the air from walrus-skin blankets. Hunters did this too, but it was not a game. Hunters would toss one hunter high into the air so that he might spot a distant herd of caribou.

One other fact might interest you about the Eskimos. They rarely spanked their children!

Fishing fleet at Homer

Today, some Eskimos still live like their great-great-grandparents. But many have gone to Alaska's cities, where they work in a wide variety of jobs.

The Aleut Indians called Alaska "The Great Land." The Aleuts lived (and some 2,000 still live) on the cold, foggy Aleutian (ah • LOO • shen) Islands, which were named for them.

The Aleuts killed giant whales with poisoned harpoons. They wore hooded coats called *parkas*. They lived in underground houses. The walls were made out of wood and whale bones. The roof was made of dirt and grass.

VITUS BERING

For thousands of years the Aleuts, Eskimos, and other people of Alaska lived as they had for generations. Then, outsiders came. Everything changed.

The Russians were the first outsiders. Vitus Bering (VIE•tiss BAIR•ing) is thought to be the first explorer. On July 16, 1741, Bering landed on an Alaskan island.

On the trip home, Bering's ship was wrecked. Vitus Bering died. But some of his sailors made it back to Russia. They carried some rich furs with them—from an animal called the sea otter. A single sea otter fur once sold for $2500. Rich people around the world were willing to pay a lot of money for sea otter fur.

Alaska was claimed by Russia, largely because of the sea otters. Russian fur traders killed sea otters by the thousands. It was easy. Sea otters are playful, gentle animals. The fur traders also killed thousands of fur seals. The seals came every year to have their babies on the Pribilof (PRIB•ih•loff) Islands (also called the Seal Islands).

Pribilof Island fur seals

The Russian fur traders made the Aleut Indians kill sea otters for them. The Aleuts did not want to be Russian slaves. They fought the Russians, and once burned four of their ships. For revenge the Russians killed thousands of Aleuts.

This was one of the saddest periods of Alaskan history. The white snow of "The Great Land" was turned red with the blood of people and animals.

Alexander Baranov (BAIR•ah•noff) was the leader of the Russian fur traders. He made Sitka (SIT•kah) their capital in 1806. Stores, schools, churches, and hospitals were built in Sitka and other Russian settlements.

The Russians were in Alaska because of the sea otters and fur seals. But they killed too many. A time came when there were almost *no* animals left.

Left: Folk dancers in Sitka wearing traditional Russian costumes

Above: A view of Sitka

This was when Russia decided to sell Alaska to the United States. In 1867, Russia named its price. "For ten million dollars you can buy Alaska!" they said.

The American Secretary of State at the time was William H. Seward (SOO•ward). "We'll buy Alaska for seven million, two hundred thousand dollars!" said Seward. The deal was made. The American flag was raised over Alaska. Alaska wasn't a state. It was owned by the United States. Sitka remained its capital.

Most Americans thought that Seward had made a foolish deal. They called Alaska "Seward's Folly," "Seward's Icebox," and "Icebergia."

For the next thirty years the United States paid little attention to Alaska. Some people came to Alaska to fish for salmon. Others hunted. A few searched for gold. It was lucky for the wildlife that few outsiders were there. The sea otters, once nearly wiped out, began to grow in numbers. The numbers of fur seals began to grow, too.

In 1896, gold was found in the Klondike (KLON•dike) area of Canada, very near Alaska. The Gold Rush to Canada began. In order to get to the gold fields of Canada, many people passed *through* Alaska. Alaskan towns such as Skagway and Wrangell grew.

In 1899, gold was discovered at Nome (NOHM), in Alaska. Over 40,000 people went to Nome's golden beaches. Then in 1902, gold was found in Fairbanks.

A pan of gold nuggets

Skagway

The sea otter had brought the Russians to Alaska. But it was gold that brought the Americans. For the next fifteen years gold was found in many places in Alaska. The gold miners became known as "sourdoughs." This was because they used a sour dough to make biscuits. Some sourdoughs got rich. Most didn't. For one thing, it cost a lot to live there. Supplies had to be shipped long distances. Eggs cost $20 a dozen! A glass of milk cost $5!

Many miners saw that there was more money to be made in business. They opened stores. They opened restaurants. Others became the carpenters and bricklayers. Fishing became a big business.

During the early 1900s Juneau (JOO•noh), Fairbanks, and other towns grew into small cities. Juneau was made the capital of Alaska.

In 1912, a huge volcano exploded at Mount Katmai (KAT•my). On June 2 people heard the mountain rumble and fled. On June 6, the whole top of Mount Katmai blew off. This was one of the biggest volcanic explosions in history. It was heard 1000 miles away. Ashes were blown high into the sky. They blocked out the sun so that it was as dark as night. Glaciers melted. Trees and animals were killed.

The explosion made the Valley of Ten Thousand Smokes—a place where a few jets of steam still shoot from the ground. Mount Katmai and other volcanoes in

Mt. Katmai

Alaska are still active. They can explode again, at any time. Alaska has most of the active volcanoes in the United States.

That same year—1912—Alaska became territory of the United States. Now the voters in Alaska could elect their own lawmakers. But many still weren't happy.

"We want Alaska to become a state!" they said. But time after time the United States Congress refused to make Alaska a state.

In 1942, during World War II, Alaska was invaded by the Japanese. For a short time the Japanese controlled Attu and several other Aleutian Islands. American soldiers had to fight hard to get this land back in 1943.

After this, Americans realized how important Alaska was. An enemy could take over Alaska, and get into America from there. On June 30, 1958, Congress finally made Alaska our 49th state. Juneau was the capital.

In 1964 Alaska was hit by a major disaster. On March 27, Good Friday, the greatest earthquake ever recorded in North America cracked and shook The Great Land. Anchorage (ANG•ker•ije) —Alaska's biggest city— was hit very hard. Buildings toppled. Houses, cars, and people were swallowed up by huge cracks in the ground.

But the worst was yet to come. The earthquake created huge waves, called *tidal waves.* Towns near the ocean

Anchorage after the earthquake

were flooded. Valdez (val • DEEZ), Seward, and Kodiak
(KOH • dee • ack) were wrecked. Many Indian villages were
swallowed up. The tidal waves were so powerful that
three people in California, 2,000 miles away, were washed
out from the beach and drowned.

Valdez

Alaska is often called "The Last Frontier." Many Alaskans think of themselves as frontier people—people who are settling a new land. It takes more than an earthquake to break their spirits. Alaskans rebuilt Anchorage, Fairbanks, Seward, Valdez, and other cities that had been wrecked.

In 1968 a huge oil field was discovered at Prudhoe (PROOD•oh) Bay, near the Arctic (ARK•tick) Ocean. This Alaskan oil field is the biggest in North America. Oil is so valuable that it is called "black gold." Oil is needed to heat homes, run cars, and keep machinery working.

Left: A view of the Alaska pipeline

Above: Close-up of an elevated section of the pipeline

In 1973 work began on a huge pipeline. The oil would flow south along the pipeline from Prudhoe Bay to Valdez. Then it would be taken by ship to the West Coast. Thousands of people came to Alaska to build this pipeline.

In 1976 Alaskans voted to move their capital from Juneau to Willow, a city 50 miles north of Anchorage. This move is supposed to start in 1980.

A ferryliner near Juneau

A TRIP THROUGH ALASKA

You have learned about Alaska's history. Now you are ready for a trip through the state.

Begin your trip in Alaska along the "Marine Highway." This highway is not a road. It is a part of the Pacific Ocean along the southeast coast of Alaska. Ferryliners (which will carry you and your car) stop at many of the coastal cities.

Your first stop is the city of Ketchikan (KETCH • ih • can). Ketchikan only has about 7,000 people, but it is one of the state's biggest cities.

Ketchikan

Don't forget your raincoat. Ketchikan is one of the rainiest cities in the United States. It gets about 14 feet of rain a year.

Once, Ketchikan was a Tlingit Indian fishing village. Today, Ketchikan is known as the "Salmon Capital of the World." More salmon is canned here than in any other city of the world. Many Tlingit Indians work in the fish canneries.

Alaska's great forests (mostly in the south and southeast) make lumbering one of the state's greatest industries. Ketchikan has a big sawmill and a pulp mill.

The city of Sitka is a lumbering and fishing center, too. Sitka is about 185 air miles northwest of Ketchikan. It is on Baranof Island, along the Marine Highway. When the Russians had Alaska, Sitka was the capital. Even after the United States bought Alaska, Sitka stayed the capital until 1900.

Visit Sitka National Historical Park. It was here that the Russians beat the Sitka Indians in a bloody battle. Part of the city is called "Old Russian Sitka." This is what Sitka looked like during the Russian period.

Sitka

Left: St. Nicholas Russian Orthodox Church in Juneau

Above: Juneau

Juneau is almost 100 miles northeast of Sitka. Juneau began in 1880. That year, Joe Juneau and Dick Harris found gold. Soon there were enough people here to start a town — which was named after Joe Juneau.

You can't drive into Juneau. Mountains make that impossible. You can fly or take the Marine Highway.

Visit Gold Creek where gold was first spotted. A giant gold mine operated in Juneau until 1944. Finally, the cost of mining the gold became too high. The Alaska-Juneau mine had to close. You can still visit this mine, from which millions of dollars of gold were taken. There is still gold in the Juneau area.

The city of Juneau lies in a 1,216-square-mile area of glaciers called the Juneau Ice Field. A gigantic glacier, the Mendenhall (MEN•den•hall) Glacier, is near the Juneau Airport. This is a 12-mile-long mountain of ice. Because of the way the ice reflects the light, the glacier looks blue. You can get very close to the Mendenhall Glacier. But don't get *too* close. Gigantic pieces of ice often crash from the glacier.

Glacier Bay

Glacier Bay is northwest of Juneau. Do you hear those crashes that sound like thunder? Those sounds are from pieces of the glaciers falling into the Bay. These big pieces of ice are called *icebergs*.

You have visited just a small part of Alaska—the southeast. Now you are in a jet flying from Juneau to Anchorage. Anchorage is Alaska's biggest city. Almost one-third of all Alaskans live in or near Anchorage.

Anchorage was founded in 1914. That year, work began on the Alaska Railroad. It is still the headquarters of that railroad which runs between Anchorage and Fairbanks.

Anchorage is sometimes called the "Crossroads of the Air World." Big jets come and go at Anchorage International Airport. Some of these jets fly *over* the North Pole to get to Europe.

Anchorage is in the south-central part of the state. It is not nearly as cold as you may think. On most summer days the temperature is over 50°F. But in the winter, it often gets as cold as -20°F.

Anchorage

Even though it's cold then, February is a good month to visit Anchorage. That's when the Anchorage Fur Rendezvous is held. The fur trappers come to town to sell their furs—and have fun! World championship sled dog races are held. There are parades, Blanket Toss shows, and dances, too.

There isn't much farming in Alaska. The Matanuska (mat•an•OOS•kah) Valley, near Anchorage, is the state's biggest farming area. Farmers raise dairy cows, hogs, and chickens. They grow potatoes, oats, and cabbages.

Alaska has very short summers. But the summer days have long hours of sunlight. Some days the sun will shine for 20 hours! Crops grow fast and big. That is why some Alaskan farmers are able to grow 70-pound cabbages.

On a clear day in Anchorage, you can see a mountain that is 240 miles to the north. This is Mount McKinley (mih•KIN•lee). At 20,320 feet, it is the tallest mountain in North America.

Mount McKinley is in a huge park named Mount McKinley National Park. It has glaciers and many other mountains of the Alaska Range.

You can see some of Alaska's interesting animals in Mount McKinley National Park. You can see moose—the largest of the deer family. You can see caribou with towering antlers on their heads. You can watch Dall sheep climb mountains as easily as you walk up stairs. At night you may hear the howls of wolves. There are grizzly bears in the park, too.

Left: A deer
Below: Mt. McKinley

Alaska brown bear

Bald eagles

Grizzly bears are big. But they have cousins that are even bigger. These are the Alaska brown bears, which live mainly on Kodiak Island. The Kodiak bears, as they are often called, are the biggest bears *in the world.* In 1894 one was shot that weighed 1,656 pounds.

The bald eagle is Alaska's most famous bird. If you look at a dollar, you will see a bald eagle. The bald eagle is the emblem of the United States. More bald eagles live in Alaska than in the rest of the states put together.

Maybe you'll see a grizzly bear, a moose, or even a bald eagle as you take the Alaska Railroad into Fairbanks.

Fairbanks is Alaska's second biggest city. Fairbanks has a nickname—the "Heart of the Golden North." This city was built by a gold rush. On July 22, 1902, Felix Pedro (FEE•lix PAY•droh) found gold about 16 miles north of Fairbanks. As people came to pan for gold, the town grew.

Visit the Silver Fox Mine. There you can go underground and see how the gold is mined today.

Fairbanks is the main home of the University of Alaska. Visit University Museum. Here you can learn about the Eskimos and other Alaskan natives.

Fairbanks

Kotzebue

About 450 miles northwest of Fairbanks is the second
largest Eskimo village — Kotzebue (KAWT ● zuh ● byoo).
You can't drive to Kotzebue. No roads go there.
You'll have to fly. The airplane is the best way to travel
the great distances in Alaska.

"You are flying over the Yukon (YOO ● kahn) River!"
says the pilot. The Yukon is Alaska's longest river. It is
over 1400 miles long. It just about divides the state in
half.

FAIRVIEW SOUTH
LIBRARY
SKOKIE, ILLINOIS 60076

"Now you are crossing the Arctic Circle!" The Arctic Circle is an imaginary circle that surrounds the North Pole.

Kotzebue is in the Arctic—30 miles north of the Arctic Circle. Right after you land, you'll notice something. It is cold! Much colder than Fairbanks. The farther north you go, the colder it gets.

There are no trees in Kotzebue, even in the summer. Much of Alaska remains frozen all year long. This permanently frosted ground is called *permafrost.* About 60 per cent of Alaska is covered by permafrost.

No trees can grow in Kotzebue's permafrost. Most trees need water, which they can not get from this frozen ground.

Eskimo woman in Kotzebue

Kotzebue has been an Eskimo trading center for
hundreds of years. Some Eskimos still hunt and fish just
as they have for ages. They catch seals, salmon, and
whales.

If you go to Kotzebue around June 21, you'll be
surprised. It never gets dark. Why? Because of the tilt of
the Earth, the sun doesn't set. It just goes in a big circle
near the horizon. This happens in all the land north of the
Arctic Circle. That is why the Arctic is called the "Land
of the Midnight Sun."

Left: A polar bear

Above: The midnight sun

The opposite is true in winter. For a few days, the sun never rises in the Arctic.

Whales are the biggest of all Arctic animals. In 1921, a huge whale was killed in Alaska. This whale was too big to put on a scale, but it is thought that it weighed 200,000 pounds. That makes it much bigger than the biggest dinosaur.

Polar bears live in the Arctic, too. Polar bears are *usually* smaller than Kodiak bears. But in 1961, an unusually big Polar bear was shot near Kotzebue. It weighed over 2,200 pounds and was over 11 feet tall.

An Eskimo with his dog team in Kotzebue

Up until a few years ago, Alaskans in the Arctic often used sled dogs. Today, many use snowmobiles. But there are still a few places in Alaska that can only be reached by dog sleds.

In 1925, sled dogs saved many people in Nome. The people were sick with diphtheria. Some died. More would die unless they were given medicine. The problem was, the medicine was in a town hundreds of miles away. It was winter, and the temperature was -45°F. Planes in 1925 couldn't fly in such weather. The only way to get the medicine to Nome was by dog sled.

Teams of dogs pulled the medicine mile after mile through the icy land. After six days, the dogs and the medicine reached Nome. Thanks to the sled dogs, many were saved.

There are many Eskimo villages in the snow-covered Arctic. Barrow is the biggest village. It is the farthest north town in the United States.

At Barrow you can see old Eskimo igloos made of dirt and whale bones. There are so many whales in the nearby Arctic Ocean that Barrow is known as "The Whaling Capital of the World."

A whale killed by Eskimos

The Naval Arctic Research Laboratory is near Barrow. Here, scientists study the Arctic Ocean. They study the weather. They study whales, polar bears, and other animals of the Arctic.

East of Barrow along the Arctic Ocean is a flat area called the North Slope. In 1968, oil was discovered at a place called Prudhoe Bay. One day, the oil found at Prudhoe Bay may heat your house and run your car.

A sea otter

Wrangell

Alaska is a great and exciting state. It is the place
where the Indians first crossed over to America. It is the
place where the tallest mountain in America stands. It is
our biggest state.

Eskimo, Aleut and Indian villages . . .

The modern cities of Anchorage, Fairbanks, and
Juneau . . .

Sea otters, whales, polar bears . . .

Gold and oil . . .

All this can be found in The Great Land—Alaska!

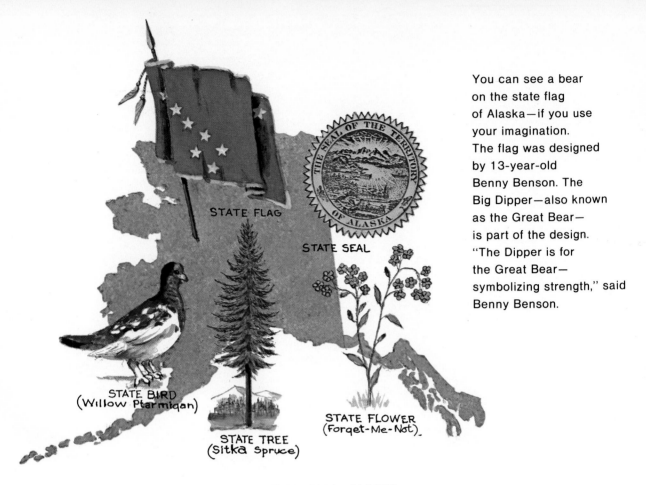

STATE FLAG

STATE SEAL

STATE BIRD
(Willow Ptarmigan)

STATE TREE
(Sitka Spruce)

STATE FLOWER
(Forget-Me-Not)

You can see a bear on the state flag of Alaska—if you use your imagination. The flag was designed by 13-year-old Benny Benson. The Big Dipper—also known as the Great Bear—is part of the design. "The Dipper is for the Great Bear—symbolizing strength," said Benny Benson.

Facts About ALASKA

Area—589,757 square miles (*the* biggest state)

Highest Point—20,320 feet above sea level (Mount McKinley, *the* highest mountain in North America)

Lowest Point—Sea level (along the shores of the Pacific Ocean)

Hottest Recorded Temperature—100°F. (in 1915, at Fort Yukon)

Coldest Recorded Temperature—minus 80°F. (in 1971, at Prospect Creek, near Barrow)

Statehood—49th state, January 3, 1959

Capital—Juneau 1900-1976—Willow chosen in 1976

Number of Boroughs—11

U.S. Senators—2

U.S. Representatives—1

Electoral Votes—3

State Senators—20

State Representatives—40

State Song—"Alaska's Flag" by Marie Drake and Elinor Dusenbury

State Motto—*North to the Future*

Origin of Name—From Aleut word "Alyeska"—meaning "The Great Land"

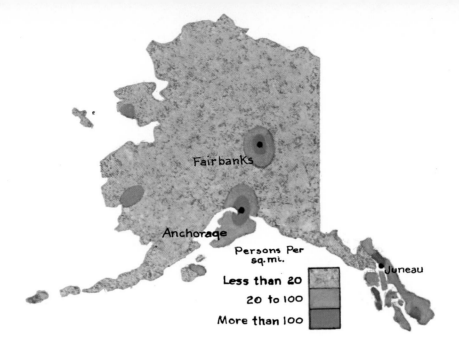

Fairbanks

Anchorage

Persons Per sq. mi.

Juneau

Less than 20
20 to 100
More than 100

Nicknames—"The Last Frontier," "Land of the Midnight Sun"

State Seal—Adopted in 1913, before Alaska was a state

State Flag—Designed by Benny Benson in 1926 and adopted in 1927, before Alaska was a state

State Flower—Forget-me-not

State Tree—Sitka spruce

State Bird—Willow ptarmigan

State Fish—King salmon

Principal Rivers—Yukon (stretches for almost 1,400 miles across state). Kuskokwim, Tanana, Susitna, Matanuska, Porcupine, Koyukuk

Some of the Animals in Alaska—Grizzly bears, Kodiak bears moose, caribou, Dall sheep, musk ox, reindeer, wolves, foxes, sea otters, walruses, seals, whales, bald eagles, ducks, geese, swans

Farm products—Milk, beef cattle, sheep, hogs, poultry, eggs, potatoes, barley, oats, cabbages

Fishing—Salmon, king crabs, scallops, shrimps, halibut cod

Mining—Oil, gold, sand, gravel, silver, mercury, platinum, uranium

Manufacturing Products—Canning and fast freezing of fish and other foods, logging, wood processing, printing, parkas, boots, and other clothing

Population—400,481 (1980 census) The state with the fewest people

Population Density—68 people for each 100 square miles (1980 census)

Major cities—Anchorage 173,017
        Fairbanks 22,645
        Juneau 19,528
        Sitka 7,803
        Ketchikan 7,198
        Kodiak 4,756

Alaska's History

Scientists think that people first came to Alaska, across the Bering Land Bridge, more than 20,000 years ago. Eskimos are believed to have sailed to Alaska about 10,000 years ago.

1728—Vitus Bering sails through Bering Strait for the Russian Czar, proving that Asia and America are not connected

1741—Bering lands on Alaskan soil on July 16

1784—First Russian settlement is founded, on Kodiak Island

1799—Russia claims Alaska

1806—Sitka becomes capital of Russian America

1867—United States buys Alaska, on March 30

1878—Salmon canning industry begins in Alaska

1880—Gold! Found at Juneau by Joe Juneau and Dick Harris

1892—Reindeer brought from Siberia to help feed Eskimos and Indians

1896—Gold is found in Canada's Klondike area; Alaska's towns grow as prospectors stop there on the way to Canada

1899—Gold found at Nome

1900—Juneau named capital.

1902—Gold found at Fairbanks

1911-1912—U. S. passes laws to protect sea otters and fur seals

1912—Alaska officially becomes a U. S. territory

1912—Mount Katmai has great volcanic explosion

1914—City of Anchorage founded as headquarters for Alaska Railroad

1923—Alaska Railroad completed

1942—Alaska Highway is completed

1942—Alaska is invaded by the Japanese

1943—Japanese driven out of Alaska

1958—Statehood for Alaska is approved by Congress, on June 30

1959—President Eisenhower signs proclamation making Alaska the 49th state, on January 3; Juneau is the capital of the new state

1963—Marine Highway opens

1964—Good Friday Earthquake, greatest earthquake ever recorded in North America, on March 27

1967—Flood in Fairbanks, in August

1968—Huge oil field is discovered on North Slope, at Prudhoe Bay

1971—Congress gives $962.5 million and 40 million acres of land to settle Eskimo and Indian land claims

1973—Construction begins on Alaska pipeline, designed to transport oil from Prudhoe Bay to Valdez

1974—Alaskans vote to make a new capital nearer to the center of the state

1976—Willow chosen as new capital

1978—Jay S. Hammond is elected to a second term as governor

1980—U.S. lawmakers designate 104 million acres of Alaska as wildlife refuges and other kinds of federal lands

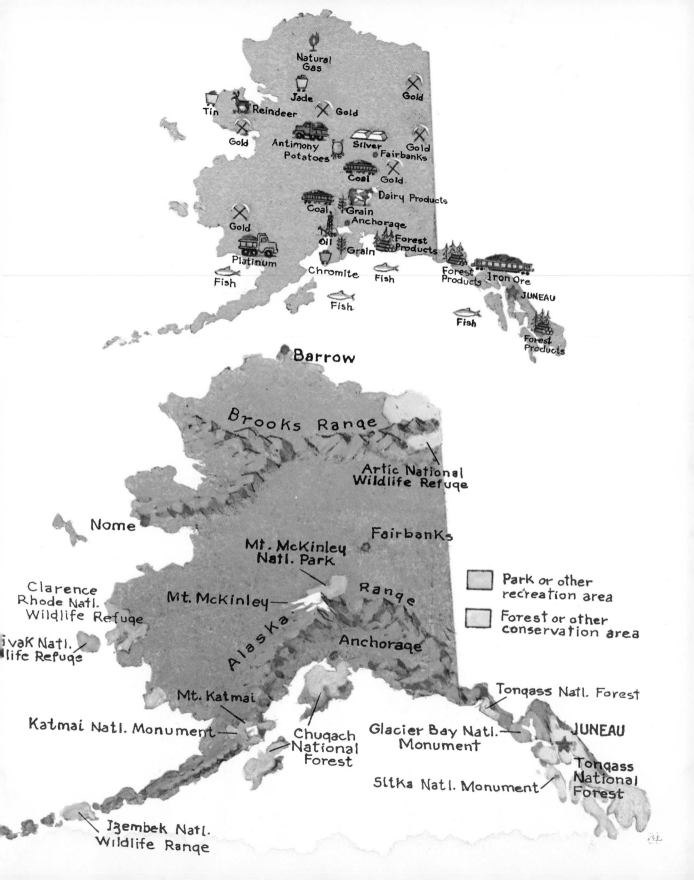

Top map (resource map):

Natural Gas

Jade

Gold

Tin

Reindeer

Gold

Gold

Antimony

Silver

Gold

Potatoes

Fairbanks

Coal

Gold

Dairy Products

Gold

Coal

Grain

Anchorage

Oil

Grain

Forest Products

Platinum

Chromite

Fish

Forest Products

Iron Ore

Fish

Fish

JUNEAU

Fish

Forest Products

Bottom map (parks and geography):

Barrow

Brooks Range

Artic National Wildlife Refuge

Nome

Fairbanks

Mt. McKinley Natl. Park

Clarence Rhode Natl. Wildlife Refuge

Mt. McKinley

Alaska Range

ivak Natl. life Refuge

Anchorage

Mt. Katmai

Tongass Natl. Forest

Katmai Natl. Monument

Chugach National Forest

Glacier Bay Natl. Monument

JUNEAU

Sitka Natl. Monument

Tongass National Forest

Izembek Natl. Wildlife Range

Legend:

Park or other recreation area

Forest or other conservation area

INDEX

About the Author:

Dennis Fradin attended Northwestern University on a creative writing scholarship and graduated in 1967. While still at Northwestern, he published his first stories in *Ingenue* magazine and also won a prize in *Seventeen's* short story competition. A prolific writer, Dennis Fradin has been regularly publishing stories in such diverse places as *The Saturday Evening Post, Scholastic, National Humane Review, Midwest,* and *The Teaching Paper.* He has also scripted several educational films. Since 1970 he has taught second grade reading in a Chicago school—a rewarding job, which, the author says,"provides a captive audience on whom I test my children's stories." Married and the father of two children, Dennis Fradin spends his freetime with his family or playing a myriad of sports and games with his childhood chums.

About the Artist:

Robert Ulm, a Chicago resident, has been an advertising and editorial artist in both New York and Chicago. Mr. Ulm is a successful painter as well as an illustrator. In his spare time he enjoys fishing and playing tennis.